365 Days
of
Writing Fiction

Charlotte Hopkins

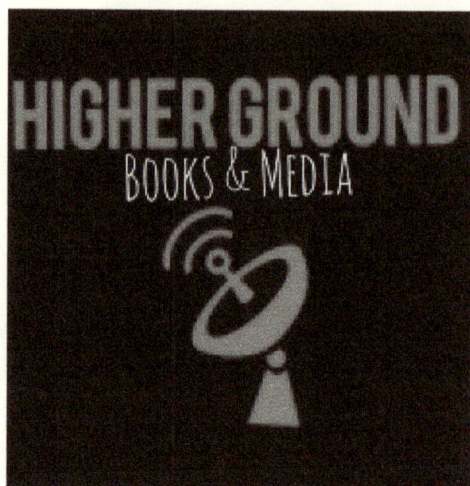

Unless otherwise noted, all Scripture quotations are from the Holy Bible, New King James Version. Copyright © 1979, 1980, 1982, 1995.

Higher Ground Books & Media
Springfield, Ohio.
http://highergroundbooksandmedia.com

Printed in the United States of America 2019

365 Days
of
Writing Fiction

Charlotte Hopkins

DEDICATION

With a special thanks to Denise DeCecco, Dottie Shearer, Sandra Shreck, Colleen Yaiser, Jan Green, and Walt Pietschmann for always being there for me.

To a special group of writers Sophie Heng, Julia Press Simmons, Liz DeJesus, Yolanda Lynx Holmes, Kelly Bostedo-Arlia, and Terri Quick

As always, a special dedication to Justin and Megan

INTRODUCTION

Are you looking for fresh ideas for your writing? Want to add flair to your writing style? Does writer's block have you wracking your brain for new story lines? With a timeline of 365 Days of creative writing prompts, you can fill all of those needs and generate a writer's bank chock full of new stories.

Whether you are looking to start the new year off with a creative twist to your writing plan or picking things up in the middle of the year, these ideas are just what you need to add spark to your writing days. Create new worlds and shake things up with fiction ideas that will keep you writing all year. Get your pen in hand – it is time to write!

JANUARY

January 1: Write at least one page a day. At the end of the year you will have a 365 page book!

January 2: Write the names of 5 relatives that you never met. Now, write a profile of each.

January 3: Write about the contents of a lady's purse.

January 4: A little girl is looking for the best hillside to go sled riding. What are her adventures for that day?

January 5: Find a picture of a bird and write a children's story about a city bird that visits his brother in the country.

January 6: A group of friends are gathering together to make the "best pot of chili ever" to compete at a chili cook-off! They each add something special – why is it special?

January 7: A teen spends the day volunteering at an animal shelter as an assignment for school.

January 8: A group of young mothers (or middle aged women) form the Teacup Society. They hold monthly meetings to compare and taste a variety of favorite teas and have discussions that lead to so much more than "what they think of the new blackberry licorice tea that they flavor with cherry juice instead of honey!"

January 9: A restaurant cook is having a terrible day and looking forward to coming home to the soup that is slowly cooking in a crock pot! It's not a typical soup, it's one created from leftovers in the fridge. An unexpected guest also arrives!

January 10: A battered wife leaves her husband and child. She comes back 3 years later for her daughter and discovers that Family Services removed her daughter from the father's home. She has since been adopted by a family that relocated to another state. No one is willing to help her locate her daughter and has to find a way to do it on her own.

January 11: Now, the tables have turned, a husband is abused by his wife. Shame keeps him from seeking help. When he does try, no one listens to him.

January 12: Write about a psychologist whose specialty is helping people to combat fears. He just started helping 4 new people with fears of water, spiders, clowns, and peanut butter!

January 13: A radio DJ is giving love advice and because stalked by a caller who fell in love with her voice.

January 14: Choose a picture of any animal. Recreate that animal into a person. What does the animal look like as a person? What is his career, his likes and dislikes? What are his favorite foods and bad habits?

January 15: A dad who has dreams of his son playing professional football. He learns that his son has been skipping football practice to go bowling. he has his own dreams of being a professional bowler.

January 16: Open up any book, copy the first sentence from page 48 and then create a story around it.

January 17: Rewrite a fairy tale from the secondary character's point of view.

January 18: An overworked Market Research Analyst thinks he is having a heart attack and later learns it was an anxiety attack. His company insists that he takes 2 months off out of fear that he actually may have a heart attack. The first two weeks are the hardest but he slowly learns to enjoy the time with his family and to reorganize his priorities (with a few twists and bumps along the way).

January 19: A man in church is given a homemade remedy to fight the cold he has had for over 2 weeks. During the sermon he starts to feel dizzy and goes to the lounge downstairs from the sanctuary. He lies down on the couch for a few minutes. When he wakes up, he is back in time to shortly after the church opened. The church members are telling him that his memories of taking the medicine and lying down are just a dream.

January 20: A preschool teacher, Aubreyanna, lives with the memories of her sister, Danielle, dying in a house fire when she was 4 years old. She and her parents moved away after the fire. Now that they live far away, there is no grave site for her to visit, only stories about Danielle from family members. She has a strong memory of being at the zoo with her sister and taking photographs of the giraffes. As an adult, Aubreyanna loves giraffes and has a collection to show it. Her best friend buys a giraffe painting at a yard sale as a gift for her, when she notices this message scrolled on the back: "For Aubreyanna, Love Dani! May 1998" The painting matches one of Aubreyanna's old photographs. But the date is 2 years after her sister died.

January 21: A high school student, who has dreamed of being a writer since she was 7 years old, enters a writing contest with several others in her class. The local radio station is holding a writing contest with the theme, "What the Pledge of Allegiance Means to Me." The winner will be awarded a $5,000 scholarship towards a local writing school. Twenty minutes before the deadline she learns that someone stole her story.

January 22: A housewife wins a writing contest and now has the opportunity to start her own magazine - on any subject – what will it be about? Who will advertise in it? Who will the magazine be geared towards?

January 23: A group of friends are having a sleepover when a thunderstorm rolls through town, taking out the power, knocking over trees and more. House does this shake up – or escite their slumber party?

January 24: What would it be like to live in the days of the wild west? Write from the perspective of a cigar maker, a writer, and a teacher.

January 25: A Deputy Fire Chief, put in charge of 3 groups of firefighters at chemical plants, lets the money he earns change him into a superficial person. He leaves his girlfriend, of 4 years, because she is a preschool teacher and does not make enough money, according to his new high standards. His new love is a financial director. The two marry 4 months later. Two years later he is a broken and demoted man. His new love tore his life apart. She was just as greedy as him – if not more. The only one who can, or may even want to, help him back on his feet, is his first love. The one that he left broken hearted. Will she want to help him? Will she punish him for what he did to her?

January 26: Start an idea journal. Make a list of book titles that you have been working on or would want to someday write.

January 27: A mom and daughter (100 years in the past or 100 years in the future) are making a chocolate cake for a new family in town.

January 28: A college student on break; goes camping alone. Who does she meet along the way and later at her camp site?

January 29: A mother takes in a foster child who has been in 8 previous homes. She tells her that they plan to adopt her but she doesn't believe them and takes to writing her name anywhere she can – with a sharpie!

January 30: You are talking to your great great grandmother on her death bed. What family secrets does she want to tell you?

January 31: Choose an ad from the classifieds and write a story around it.

FEBRUARY

February 1: Write an episode of one of your favorite TV shows.

February 2: Write a children's book about how Punxsutawney Phil will spend this Groundhog's Day?

February 3: A soldier, away at war, writes a love letter to his crush, that does not arrive until 23 years later. He forgot to add the zip code, sending it lost on the mail!

February 4: Write a story about getting lost in the woods on a snowy day.

February 5: A middle aged man decides to start a healthy life style. Write a story about why he made this decision and all the changes he plans to make!

February 6: A woman is walking home in extremely cold weather. Why is she walking? What happens along the way? What does she do first when she gets home?

February 7: It is February 7, 1963, the Beatles arrive in America. Write a story about that day from the mind of a security guard at the airport, one of the screaming fans, and a budding musician watching the day's events unfold on his tv at home.

February 8: A young man writes a love letter to a secret crush and it falls into the hands of the wrong girl. She thinks it is for her, and that it came from her secret crush. She accidentally drops the letter, which continues to be passed along and continues to cause misunderstandings by each person that finds it.

February 9: Two young Amish children are building a clubhouse for themselves. What are their plans for the new clubhouse? What do they do on the last day of building!

February 10: A young man in 1942 is searching for his high school sweetheart that moved away. Does he find her? How? Does it take a few months? A year? Or 20 or 30 years?

February 11: A man finds a bottle with a message inside that reads, "Hi my name is Dan! I died of cancer when I was 42 years old. I always loved to travel so please throw me back into the water." Write a story of all the journeys that the bottle will travel.

February 12: Write a story about Abraham Lincoln's life from the observations of his teacher.

February 13: Get a baby name book and open to any random page. Close your eyes and point to a name in the book. Give that name to a character in a story about someone on a bus. Where is he going? What is he doing?

February 14: A young woman gets an antique necklace as a Valentine's Day gift from her boyfriend. She then starts having dreams of herself living in the past and getting that necklace as a gift – when it was new. The dreams become more and more surreal

February 15: A 9 year old girl is in the hospital following a snowmobile accident. She soon discoveries that the hospital is haunted by the spirit of another girl. What is the spirit looking for? How can she help her? Does the spirit have an impact on her as well?

February 16: Write a story that takes place in another country. The characters of the story are a chef, a real estate agent, a security guard, and a pet shop owner.

February 17: A newly married couple embark on the task of transferring an old barn into their dream home – all the while, spending as little money as possible.

February 18: Write a fiction piece about a lesser known US President during his campaign for the White House.

February 19: Delve into writing a romance novel! Include events such as - puppy found on the side of the road, busted pipes, shopping for an antique quilt, bonfire with friends, locked outside during a thunderstorm, making a homemade pizza, and losing a job.

February 20: Write a fiction story about your parents meeting for the first time.

February 21: A group of friends set off in teams in a competition of who can collect the most autographs in 6 months – from celebrities, politicians, DJ's, and more!

February 22: A young politician in 2088 idolizes George Washington. He dreams of being president and following Washington's ideals.

February 23: Two friends find themselves rivals in a tennis match.

February 24: Write about a true love that "got away!"

February 25: Spend an afternoon bowling, watch the others who are there to bowl and make them characters in a book.

February 26: Write about missing a train!

February 27: Write the first and last page of a story that involves a fire and a car accident.

February 28: Write about someone's most prized possession – the history behind it and why it is important.

MARCH

March 1: Write a children's book of two pigs who are friends and spend the day roaming their farm – and the neighborhood!

March 2: Visit a thrift shop and buy a handful of items. Write a story that includes all your small treasures.

March 3: Write a story about friends camping out along the edge of a creek that is nestled along a walking trail.

March 4: A librarian is given the task of planning events at the library to draw more readers into the library.

March 5: Write, in the first person, about being stuck in traffic.

March 6: A single parent just moved to a new town. How will she celebrate the first day in her new home, what are her plans? What unexpected events happen to shape the day – good and bad?

March 7: Write a children's story about a ladybug that survived winter and is preparing for the first spring days with his insect friends.

March 8: A group of friends are caught up in a storm while they are out on a boat. They take shelter in an old lighthouse until they can leave safely.

March 9: An Irishman in the early 1800's is trying to find a job but the help wanted signs read, "No Irish Need Apply."

March 10: A group of friends start a Kickstarter page to raise money for a documentary about bullying.

March 11: Write a children's book about a parent and child touring an apple orchard to make homemade applesauce. What do they talk about on their outing. Where do they go? Who are they making the applesauce for? Include this fun recipe:

4 Apples – peeled, cored, and chopped
¾ cup water
¼ cup white sugar
½ teaspoon ground cinnamon

In a medium saucepan combine apples, water, sugar, and cinnamon. Cover and cook over medium heat for 15-20 minutes, or until apples are soft. Allow to cool, then mash with a fork or potato masher.

March 12: Imagine your life is a novel – write the last chapter.

March 13: A young couple with a new baby, decide to leave their jobs and start a home business. Write about their fun, unforgettable moments and all of the growing pains of their new business!

March 14: A man is being awarded by the town mayor and is even getting the "key to the city." Why is he being awarded? What did he do?

March 15: Write about an accidental invention from someone 200 years in the future!

March 16: Write down a list of all of your fears. Choose one and write a story around it.

March 17: Attend a parade and pick 3 people out of the crowd that you do not know. Write a story about the good and bad that will happen to them at the parade and how they will all eventually come to interact.

March 18: Write about your worst restaurant experience from the perspective of the chef an/or the waiter.

March 19: Write 10 things you would do if you knew the world was coming to an end in 30 days.

March 20: Write about a marriage proposal that goes awry!

March 21: Write about a chance that you wouldn't take. How would your life be different if you had done it?

March 22: Write a story of a peanut farmer's wife who sets out to show a crowd all the off-the-wall uses for peanuts.

March 23: Write about a blind date where everything goes wrong!

March 24: A small lie sets off a chain of events.

March 25: Write about an encounter with a bully.

March 26: There is a belief that we have a twin in a parallel universe that lives the exact opposite lifestyle. How does your "twin" spend their days?

March 27: If you could build a home from any type of building, what would you choose. Describe each room inside.

March 28: Turn the radio on and change the station until you hear a song playing. Leave it on and listen to the words. Write a story about the thoughts that the song provokes.

March 29: Write about being a student in Julia Child's first cooking class (before she became famous)

March 30: Write about your earliest experience at the hospital, whether it is something you remember or an experience that you only heard through stories. Write from the mindset of yourself at that age – or your parent – or even the nurse!

March 31: Write a children's story about a little girl who makes a wish upon a glass jelly bean that she finds and puts it under her pillow. When she wakes up, her dream has come true. Then she makes wishes for others and puts the jelly bean under their pillow, only to find each time that the wish has always come true. But it is not always the way they expect it to.

APRIL

April 1: Write a story about the first April Fool's Day. Create your own reason for why the holiday began.

April 2: You can interview anyone – past or present – who would you interview? What would you ask them? Now write from the opinion of the person you are interviewing. How do they answer your questions?

April 3: The building had been abandoned for 12 years but as I walked down the dusty hall, I thought _____.

April 4: Visit the library and choose a random book from the shelf. Write the title of chapter 4 from the index and write a story from that.

April 5: A student learns that they have super speed and the ability to be invisible. How did they discover this? What do they do with these powers – good, bad, and accidental?

April 6: Write an "ABC" book of fun facts in regards to a mythical creature, such as, gnomes, unicorns, or dragons." Be sure to use each letter of the alphabet. For example, "An A-Z Guide to Unicorns" would start with:

*Apples were the favorite treats of the unicorn.

*Billowy manes of unicorns were as soft and fluffy as clouds.

*Corralling unicorns is hard work because they love to play hide-and-seek.

April 7: Write poems about the Easter Bunny and send them out to greeting card companies!

April 8: Write about the day in the life of a factory worker named Karen Kay Kline, whose job it is to package cookies.

April 9: A time travel experiment that goes terribly wrong.

April 10: Two friends spend the night in front of the mall for tickets to a rock concert. Who do they meet in line? What are the conversations like?

April 11: Visit a maritime museum and write a story about a soldier's days aboard a submarine.

April 12: What is your pet peeve and why? Write a story of 2 neighbors, one of which, has this "pet peeve" and the other is trying to break them of it.

April 13: Make a list of metaphors – as many as you can think of. Now, work on how you can expand on the basic metaphors, like, "skinny as a rail" or "so hungry, I can eat a horse!"

April 14: Write about the sinking of the Titanic from the perspective of someone who did not survive.

April 15: Write a story about a young man working at the first McDonald's in 1955?

April 16: Start a club for writers. The first thing everyone should write about is the day that they knew they wanted to be a writer.

April 17: Write a story about the first family that lived in your house/apartment. What did they like about it? What did they hate about it?

April 18: Write about being in high school with your mom/dad. What would it be like to be in the same grade together? Would the two of you be friends?

April 19: Write a story from a random receipt.

April 20: Imagine being in the audience at the early Olympics. Who is there? How do the events for the day conclude.

April 21: Write a love story about a couple that meet at a karaoke bar. Maybe their meeting did not start so great!

April 22: Take the last sentence from a book and use it to start a new book.

April 23: Imagine finding a nickel on the sidewalk. Where are all of the places the nickel traveled?

April 24: Each year on Administrative Professionals Day a man travels to businesses in his community and brings a flower or a small token to all administrative workers. What made him start this tradition? Why does he continue?

April 25: Write a dialog of a phone conversation between two high school friends who reunited on Facebook and exchanged phone numbers.

April 26: A woman has a surprising break up with her boyfriend of 8 years. Her friends come over to help her through it. Now write from the guy's point of view.

April 27: Write a sequel/prequel to a classic fairy tale.

April 28: Write about landing on another planet, in another galaxy. Describe everything from when you first land.

April 29: If you had a secret life, what would it be like?

April 30: A School Resource Officer finds a note from a teen...it is a suicide note. He has to figure out who wrote the note and how he can stop them from killing themselves – if the note is even real!

MAY

May 1: A young woman gets an antique necklace as a Valentine's Day gift from her boyfriend. She then starts having dreams of herself living in the past and getting that necklace as a gift – when it was new. The dreams become more and more surreal

May 2: Two people who are enemies in the business world, get stuck in an elevator together for 2 hours.

May 3: Create your own superhero? What are its powers and how did he get them? What does he use them for? Who is his arch enemy?

May 4: If you could invent something today, what would it be?

May 5: Look up random photographs of people that you do not know. What is going on in the photos and what happened immediately afterwards?

May 6: Write about a pet that you loved and cared for as a favor for a friend.

May 7: Three children take a hot air balloon ride. What are all of the things that they see from up high?

May 8: Did you know that Albert Einstein never wore socks! Today on, "No Socks Day," write a children's book about a little girl who will not wear socks until she finds the perfect pair! Write about her search and all the crazy silly socks that she finds and the ones that friends bring her.

May 9: A woman boards the wrong train and falls asleep as the trip begins. Where is she when she wakes up? Who does she meet? How does she get back home?

May 10: Write a story from the mindset of the first passengers on the Transcontinental Railroad? Where are they going? What are their plans for when they reach their destinations?

May 11: An old school has been abandoned for many years. Now when anyone enters the school it takes them back in time.

May 12: Practice writing limericks!

May 13: With May being the month that we celebrate Mother's Day, write a short story about a young woman in the 60"s who finds herself alone and pregnant after her husband dies in the war. And on a happier note, write a story about a mom today who is celebrating "motherhood" by having a picnic at a lake with a group of moms and their families. The moms reminisce about the good and bad moments of being a mommy!

May 14: Write a story about being lost in a new town! Who helps you find your way around?

May 15: A woman wakes up in the hospital with no memory of who she is. Create a story around her. Her identity, her family and her life before the accident.

May 16: The window washers at Children's Hospitals dress up as superheroes. Write about how a day at work for them.

May 17: Mallory is putting together a gift basket for her friend, Clara, in the hospital. Before Mallory leaves for her visit she makes a few stops. At each stop, others add items to the gift basket. What things get added and why? How does the visit go?

May 18: Imagine taking an Iphone and traveling back in time to show Alexander Graham Belle just how far his discovery will go. What does he think about it?

May 19: Write about what was it like to be at the Ringling Brothers circus in 1884. Write from the perspective of the families in attendance and the workers of the circus.

May 20: Write about what thoughts the word "depressed" brings on for you.

May 21: Tell the story of a man who writes inspirational messages on stacks of post-its and passes them out to friends, family and people in the neighborhood.

May 22: A waitress from a small town, who just became a single mother, wins the lottery.

May 23: A dad and his son are saving money in a jar. What are they saving up for?

May 24: Write about being confined in bed with a broken leg. What are all of the comforts of life that you would want with you? Who are the guests that come by to cheer you up?

May 25: Two friends become lost on a mountain highway and then their car breaks down. What steps do they take to stay safe in the extreme heat/cold until they can be rescued?

May 26: This is National Paper Airplane Day. Write a children's book of a child that makes a paper airplane and before he sends it sailing through the sky, he makes a wish Write about all the places that the paper airplane travels to.

May 27: A teen couple at their senior prom make plans to go to a hotel for their first romantic encounter. When they get to the hotel the girl changes her mind. She feels like she let her date down but he make the night magical for her still.

May 28: Write the names of 5 relatives that you never met. Now, write a small biography for each of them.

May 29: A child shopping at a yard sale with his mom finds a music box that releases a genie when the song is finished playing. What does she ask for with her 3 wishes? She then learns that after the third wish she has to pass the music box on to someone outside of her family. Who does she choose.

May 30: You wake up from a nightmare and go to the kitchen for a glass of water. All the furniture is changed, even the year is different. Then you hear a child call out, "Mom...."

May 31: Write about a football player still living in his glory days.

JUNE

June 1: A teacher at an all boy's school decides to take his class outdoors since it is a warm day. He notices that one of his students fell asleep. He and the class decide to play a trick on him. They quietly sneak out of the classroom. When they return the student is gone? Where did he go? Do they find him? When?

June 2: Write a story about a fruit vendor who has a small stand on the side of the road. Where is she from? What is a day in her life like?

June 3: Visit an aquarium and watch the fish. Notice how some almost take on a personality. Choose a few of the fish and write a children's book with those fish as the characters.

June 4: A mother has grand plans for her daughter's upcoming wedding but the daughter gets frustrated and insists that she doesn't want any of it. As good as her mother's intentions are, she wants something simple. She even asks that people bring simple gifts, nothing grand or expensive. As a surprise, her mother decides her to present her with a "simple wedding gift." It is a homemade cook book. With family cooking tips, secrets and recipe collections!

June 5: Write about working at a call center and dealing with angry anxious people all day! How do the colleagues morally support each other through the day – the funny times and the difficult times?

June 6: Brittany is working as a secretary at a physician's office and learns that her friend, Annie, is having a family catastrophe. Annie's younger sister was murdered. Annie friend works at a daycare center and she needs to take off work for a month but her boss said he just cannot hold her position for her. Brittany's boss agrees to let Brittany fill in for Annie and he will hold her job for her. At the daycare Brittany learn that one of the children, Conner, is from a foster home. Conner will not open up to his foster parents or the social workers. They send him to the daycare thinking that the other children will help him to open up but it does not work - until Brittany gets there. Brittany is the only one he opens up to – and the only one he learns to trust.

June 7: Write a story about a middle-aged man searching for a job after the company he has been with for 12 years, closes their doors.

June 8: A 17 year old girl, who is 6 month's pregnant, learns that her boyfriend is killed in a motorcycle accident.

June 9: Write a story about a woman who sent an email to a man by mistake when she typed in the wrong email address. The two have since become close friends – online. (different ages, backgrounds, and incomes)

June 10: If you could make a chain of vending machines that sold items other than candy and pop; what would they sell?

June 11: Write about your dream job/jobs (You can have more than one!) How does your day start and end?

June 12: A man is willed a time capsule made by his great great grandparents. It inspires him to make a time capsule for his own great great grandchildren.

June 13: A 12-year old boy is repeatedly getting into trouble. His parents and the police arrange for him to do community service on a horse ranch. Their intentions are for him to learn work ethic but the ranch family teaches him more than that – they teach him about life, dreams – and consequences.

June 14: What would you find in the computer history of your favorite author?

June 15: A family is on their way to a picnic at a lake. As they are driving along, traffic comes to a standstill. There was a landslide ahead and they are stuck in a row of cars. People are getting out of their cars and just sitting on their hoods or walking around and waiting for the traffic to start moving. Describe the other drivers and what they are doing.

June 16: The 3rd Sunday of June is Father's Day! Write about a dad whose baby is born two months before Father's Day but he cannot celebrate because he is in the military and stationed overseas. How do his fellow soldiers help him and the other military dads to celebrate their special day? And on a happier note, write about a dad who celebrates his day with a surprise visit from his daughter and grandchildren. What creative activities do they have planned for him?

June 17: Armed with a new camera, a young girl sets out to explore the community that she just moved to.

June 18: Write a series of "the one that got away," stories.

June 19: A firefighter has an after death experience.

June 20: A teen girl is kidnapped and locked in a closet. She has her cell phone in her pocket. She can't call out because she will alert to the kidnappers that she has her phone with her. So, she starts posting messages to facebook for help, as a way to reach out to as many as possible!

June 21: A teen and his first tasks of saving money. What is he saving for (besides a car)?

June 22: Write about a child's first time away at summer camp.

June 23: Two friends have an argument that is started from a misunderstood text message.

June 24: A small town holds their first carnival which includes pig races and contests for the most creative cookies and slurpies.

June 25: A young girl visits the beach with her family. She can wade in the water but cannot go swimming because she has a broken wrist and is wearing a cast. She spends her time collecting seashells and treasures in the sand. What all does she find?

June 26: Write about the last 60 years of Kennywood (or your local amusement park), including, clothing styles, snacks, rides, activities and tragedies. Write as if it were being told to you from a grounds keeper who worked there for 60 years!

June 27: A student tracing his family tree, as a school project, learns that his grandmother was adopted. She had a brother who was killed in foster care. She refused to ever talk about that day. He does his own investigation to find out what happened.

June 28: Write a children's story about the astrological signs.

June 29: A nun wants to leave the ministry. What is the new life that she wants and how does she achieve this?

June 30: A corrupt politician hires a psychic. What does he utilize the psychic for?

JULY

July 1: Write about the activities of an ice cream scientist. What flavors does he create and why? His goal is to start a new specialty line of flavors. What will they be?

July 2: Write a story about the days in the life of Betsey Ross after she was given the task of making a flag for the new country. What are some of her ideas? Talk about the visitors at her home and the friends who stop her on the road to give their opinions.

July 3: What are the ups and downs in the day-in-the-life of a hot dog street vendor in New York? What unusual things go on around them everyday?

July 4: This is the birthday of the United States, referred to as "Independence Day," as we won our independence from England. America is also referred to as "the melting pot," since immigrants from countries around the world came here to join this new nation. Many of them came through, Ellis Island. Write about that time through the eyes of a young man from Germany arriving at Ellis Island. What was the journey like? What were his "American dreams?" What is his new life as an American like?

July 5: Write about your favorite event in American history as if you were there.

July 6: Select an unusual course that is taught at college. Tell the story around the students taking the class and their eccentric professor.

July 7: A 14 year old boy is preparing to participate in his first bike race.

July 8: A newspaper reporter goes undercover at a nightclub. What is he looking for?

July 9: A man finds a bucket list in the pages of an old Bible that belonged to his dad. His mother tells him that his father wrote the list in high school. He sets out to complete the list for his dad and he learns a few family secrets along the way.

July 10: Create a children's story of teddy bears (different sizes and colors) that gather together every year, in a special spot, to celebrate Teddy Bear Picnic Day.

July 11: A police officer writes a book about the craziest stories of excuses that people had for speeding – some of them turned out to be true – bizarre but true!

July 12: Write a first person monologue of someone stuck at the top of a ferris wheel.

July 13: A group of "computer geeks" gather twice a month for a club meeting. What are their backgrounds? Create characters who do not all fit the stereotype of geek. What are some of the off-the-wall subjects that get brought up?

July 14: Spend the day working in a flower garden or just visiting several decorative gardens. Then write a story about miniature families/friends that would live in the garden.

July 15: Gather a variety of figurines. Give them names and personalities. How would they live in a community together? Are they friends, relatives, or neighbors who do not always get along?

July 16: Write a story around your favorite urban legend.

July 17: A pet owner realizes that his dog leaves the house every night at 8:00. He decides to start following him. What does he learn about where his dog is going?

July 18: Keep a diary as a teen aged girl in 1962 who wants to fly airplanes – a task that is considered "a man's job."

July 19: A zoo keeper who brings her deaf son to work with him and learns that the dolphins can understand his sign language.

July 20: Write about the day in the life of a New York cab driver compared to a cab driver in a small Nebraska town.

July 21: Write about a small specialty bookshop owner. What books does he specialize in and describe your customer base (the good and the bad).

July 22: A teen is preparing to enter a boat race and is learning everything he can about boating. His best friend is helping him, or so he thinks. It turns out the friend is trying to sabotage him. Why? How?

July 23: A young man delivering pizza to a new town gets lost and goes to the wrong house. The young lady, that answers the door, dies help him find the right house. He falls in love at first sight. What excuse does he use to go back? What is his plan to try and win her heart?

July 24: Write a story about being the sole survivor of an airplane crash.

July 25: You have been given the authority to start a new holiday. What would it be called? How would you celebrate?

July 26: A woman learns that her daughter is going to marry the son of a man who verbally bullied and humiliated her in high school. She is not sure if she should tell her daughter or if she even wants this young man in her family. The father is hoping that she doesn't remember how he treated her, or at least won't hold a grudge about it.

July 27: A young girl at a new school is wanted in the "clicks" of the "popular" girls and the "nerds." She tries to be friends with all of them but learns who her "real friends" are among them. Could it be one of the clicks or a few from both?

July 28: A teen boy has the battle of his life when he learns that his ex-girlfriend is pregnant with his baby and wants to have an abortion. He only has a short window of time to try and stop it from happening and save their baby.

July 29: A woman moves across the country. When she pulls her moving van into the driveway of her new home she finds a stowaway in the back. He is the son of her former neighbor, who was an abusive alcoholic. He begs her not to send him back.

July 30: A librarian finds a box of journals in an old storage closets. They belonged to a secret society who used to hold meetings at the library over 100 years ago. What does she discover? What does she do with this new-found information?

July 31: A woman hires a surrogate mother. During the pregnancy, she learns that the woman is her sister that was put up for adoption two years before she was born.

AUGUST

August 1: An alcoholic has that "wake up" call to put herself on the path of sobriety? What does life hold for her? How does she discover who her friends are as opposed to who just used her – and who will crash her sober life?

August 2: Two friends find themselves unemployed and decide to start a baking company. They begin by holding bake sales (like flea markets). Where does their business grow – or change – from there?

August 3: Spend the day at the airport and write a story about the most interesting people you see there. The plot of the story is of airline passengers who get locked in the lounge when bad weather sweeps in, canceling flights and knocking out the power.

August 4: A teen girl discovers that she has the power to change herself into any person that she wants to be. How does she use this new power?

August 5: A step father of a 6 year old boy learns that his wife is killed in a car accident. He decides to adopt the boy so that his father's family does not try to take him back at any time in the future. He learns that he was kidnapped as a baby. Who did she kidnap him from and why? Will he be forced to return him, even though he is the only father he knows and his only "family" left in the world?

August 6: A woman treating herself to a pedicure overhears a conversation, in which her husband's name is said, several times. She continues to listen in and before she can ask the ladies about it; they leave the salon. How does the wife overreact? What does she have in store for her husband?

August 7: A young artist visits a beach everyday for over 2 weeks and while he fills sketch books of drawings he witnesses a murder. He draws images of the murderers and the victims. When the police investigate there is no sign of a death and no missing person reports have been made. How does he uncover what he knows he witnessed, when the police won't listen?

August 8: You attend a Pittsburgh porch party! Write about how the day goes.

August 9: A teen who finds herself an outcast meets a new friend in an unusual place – a boy who feels like just as much of an outcast. How do they help each other through the awkward stages of life?

August 10: A struggling writer finds herself alone and a single mother after her husband leaves her for another woman. She struggles to pursue her writing dream hitting one road block after another, all the while she is also struggling to work and keep her small family together.

August 11: Write about being king/queen of a country that is as big as Rhode Island. What would it be like there? What does the flag look like? What are the landmarks and culture? What are the favorite foods? Do they have a specific style of clothes or slang?

August 12: An out-of-work comedian enlists the aid of a writer to help him get back on top.

August 13: A woman in the process of moving to another state, puts her things in storage. She gets sick with pneumonia and is hospitalized. It gets worse and she almost dies. She is in a coma for 3 months. When she awakens she learns that they are going to auction off her unit. She tries to contact the unit but the manager avoids her; once he realizes he can make more money through an auction than by what she owes, thanks to "Storage Wars!" She is released from the hospital 2 weeks later but not in time to save her storage unit. She spends the next 18 months trying to track down any of the items that were taken out from under her.

August 14: Take your favorite line from a film and use that as a title to a story.

August 15: If you had the opportunity to go anywhere in the world, where would you go? Write about what that trip would be like.

August 16: Two fishermen in Alaska find a rusty hour glass. One of them decides to keep it on his desk and his wife offers to take it to get it cleaned. She learns that it is not a type of metal that is used today, in fact, no one can identify the metal. She puts it back on his desk and they soon realize that it can be used to turn back the hours.

August 17: A mother of two teens, first loses her job and then her husband when he leaves her for her best friend. To support her family she starts a catering service making and delivering lunches, as well as, making lunches for school children. She runs into an old friend who begins to offer moral support. What triumphs and trials are ahead for her?

August 18: A single mom sends her 11 year old daughter to spend the summer with a father that she has not seen since she was 7 years old. The father and stepmother convince her to stay with them, since they have a large home, swimming pool and enough money to buy her what she needs. Her mother struggles to keep her relationship with her daughter and to show her daughter that she still loves her regardless of her father "buying" her away. She writes a book for her, titled, "Letters to a Lost Daughter."

August 19: Three college friends form a "Prepper Group" and tour different areas and cities to teach people how to survive in a disaster.

August 20: A writer visits a VA hospital and plans to go back every day for a year. He keeps a blog of everything the soldiers teach him and all their experiences that they want to share.

August 21: Think of a party. Who is there? Are they happy? Are some of them depressed and there to try and cheer up? How do they interact?

August 22: A firefighter breaks his leg in 2 places and is unable to work for 12 weeks. Not being able to walk much he decides to find things to do around the home. He considers writing a book. One day while trying to make something different for lunch he find how much fun it can be to create things in the kitchen. His book idea is born – it will be "101 careers created in the kitchen!"

August 23: A couponer becomes obsessed with couponing and soon has a follower that want to learn her tricks of shopping!

August 24: A couple, who learn they are unable to have children, decide to purchase a large abandoned church and transform it into a "club" for teens who need mentoring and assistance from problems at school and home to spiritual questions to questions about hobbies, careers and pets - everything in between!

August 25: A man takes on a 2nd job. he will be writing for an advice column - "Just Ask Julie!" He is sworn to privacy because the newspaper does not want anyone to know that a man is writing it. Before he can tell his wife about it, he discovers that she is writing for advice on how to deal with a husband that she feels doesn't love her anymore – and how his best friend is urging her to leave him.

August 26: A shy 8 year old confides into her reverend that she has seen Jesus and talks to him. The reverend is not sure if he believes her which makes the girl feel bad and she decides not to come back to church. Two years later the reverend is relocated. He is haunted by the memories of the little girl who did not know what to do about being able to talk to Jesus. He goes back only to find out that they too have moved away. He sets out to find her and to learn whether she truly did talk to Jesus or imagined it.

August 27: Compare the differences in a family from 1860 doing their back-to-school shopping, compared to a family from 1960, 1980 and today - 2013.

August 28: A group of friends decide to open a country bar!

August 29: Your seven year old has the day off from school because of a water main break. You decide to call off work and spend a special day doing a string of random activities. Write about how things occur.

August 30: Start a Character Journal. Include lists of names, cities, streets and careers.

August 31: Write a story about attending a Mystery Dinner Theater.

SEPTEMBER

September 1: A baker is holding an event to save himself from claiming bankruptcy. Describe how the day goes!

September 2: You have been given the task of making an "All Kids Menu" for a new restaurant. What will you serve? What will you add to the restaurant to make dining fun for kids?

September 3: Two friends (a boy and girl) decide not to go to college and opt for using their college funds to become storm chasers across the country in an attempt to write a book: Nature's Best and Scariest Moments.

September 4: Write about a freelance Art Therapist. What are her days like? Who are her clients?

September 5: An elite golf course drains their lake. What all do they find?

September 6: Three friends form a collector's club! What do they collect? What activities do they have planned? How does their club grow?

September 7: Write a story about a teen that learns his best friend is actually an alien? How did he find out? What all does he reveal?

September 8: The mayor asks you to create a new annual festival for your community. What will you plan for the big day? What will the festival be devoted to? Be creative!

September 9: A chocolate tester is creating a new candy bar. What will the creation be? How will they promote the new candy?

September 10: A doctor diagnoses a pizza driver with a terminal illness that will leave him with only 60 days to live. He feels that he has not lived a very full life so his friends plan a living funeral for him, without telling him. A few days before the living funeral he learns that he is not going to die; that there was a mistake in the blood work. His friends are still going through with the living funeral, which truly changes his life. There are some good and even a few disappointing changes ahead.

September 11: Three neighbors feud for the coveted "Golden Tulip" award, given for the best garden.

September 12: A group of men are playing a basketball game. When they are done, they get into a discussion of the history of basketball, including how it got its start. This turns into another discussion of their own ideas for a new sport.

September 13: A 3rd grade student is being home schooled. Why is he not attending public school and how does he spend the day?

September 14: In the tv series, "Quantum Leap," Sam was a scientist who got lost in time from an experiment gone wrong. He spent years leaping through history trying to fix the wrongs in the world. The show ended with Sam never leaping back home. A tv special that all Quantum Leap fans waited for. Write that episode!

September 15: Write about a man working at the patent office in 1910. What types of people does he interact with? Now write about a woman working in the patent office today and the people that she meets daily.

September 16: A high powered attorney in New York City learns that she is pregnant. Her husband is a college professor at NYU. After witnessing a mugging that bystanders don't seem to be surprised by, she he is worried about raising her daughter in the big city. She convinces her husband to move to a small town in Ohio. She takes a long leave of absence from practicing law and her husband transfers to an Ohio college. She is in for quite a surprise in the differences between the city and a small town life.

September 17: A 13-year-old girl is called down to the principal's office to answer a phone call. The phone call is from her mother – the biological mother that she was told died 4 years ago! Why did her father and step mother tell her that she died? What is she returning now?

September 18: Write about the days in the life of a child's old metal lunch box.

September 19: A young girl signs up to be an exchange student and spends a year in England.

September 20: A teen boy who has his first heartbreak is invited to a bonfire to try and cheer him up. What do they do there? What do they talk about?

September 21: A woman bakes cookies once a month for a domestic violence shelter and spends the day playing with the children and talking to the mothers. She was once in an abusive relationship and tries to give advice and most importantly moral support. One afternoon she meets a new mother and her 2 children at the shelter. The woman looks a lot like her, in fact, she is her twin sister!

September 22: A child walking through the park gets caught in a rain storm. He sits down under a tree for shelter from the rain and then falls asleep. He is woken by a chatty squirrel and discovers that the animals can talk and play but only for an hour after the rain stops.

September 23: A children's story about a butterfly, ladybug, and bumble bee who are best friends decide to have a picnic for their whole bug city – Chrissyville!

September 24: While on a camping trip with the boy scouts, a 10 year old boy learns that he can talk to animals.

September 25: A baby is abandoned at a train station. Who finds him? Who adopts him? How does he later, as an adult, use social media as a means to find out what happened that day?

September 26: A woman plans an extravagant wedding and the morning of her wedding she learns that her fiancé has been having an affair with one her cousin, the maid-of-honor, and she is pregnant. She calls off the wedding and invites a homeless shelter to enjoy the food and music that would have been her reception. She then learns that one of the women at the homeless shelter is her best friend from high school. She invites her onto the cruise that would have been her honeymoon so they can rebuild their friendship and reconnect. Write about how the events unfold.

September 27: A children's story of a young boy who takes his paintbrush through town to add color in different places.

September 28: A hotel event planner leaves her position to become a birthday party planner for children and teens.

September 29: A young woman joins a military support group and "adopts" a US soldier in the Middle East – her obligation is to make care packages and send him letters of support.

September 30: A notable fashion designer with a reputation for high quality learns that her now 14-year old daughter has also chosen to design dresses – for Barbie! How does she react? Does she help her?

OCTOBER

October 1: Marley loses everything in a house fire but is happy that her family made it out alive. Days later her husband, Mark, leaves her and their son, Aaron. How can Marley's best friend, Clayra, help her to start her life over.

October 2: You are walking down a dark street and you turn around to see...

October 3: A reporter and a group of Paranormal Investigators, spend the weekend in a haunted house, to debunk the stories of it being haunted. The house was once a hospital in the Civil War. What facts and myths do they learn of the house's history? Is it truly haunted?

October 4: A girl discovers on her 12th birthday that she is a witch, something that her 14 year old friend (who is also a witch) has known her whole life! How do they help each other to understand and control their Wiccan powers?

October 5: A group of firefighters take over an abandoned fire hall – that is legend to be haunted!

October 6: A woman gets a box of tarot cards meant to be a fun gift but she learns that she actually can read the future. She is then haunted by dreams of deceased people who want her to relay messages. What other surprises does the spirit world have for her?

October 7: An Arachnologist visits schools and museums to teach kids about spiders.

October 8: You wake up and there is a picture in your phone of you sleeping. You live alone.

October 9: A bowling alley starts a Zombie Bowling Team to bring back customers. It works out bigger and better than they could have imagined!

October 10: A 32 year old man saves the life of a witch's daughter. She thanks him with a spell that will allow everything that he asks for in the next 24 hours to come true. But warns him to be careful what he asks for!

October 11: Your wife wakes you up in the middle of the night to tell you there is an intruder in the house. But she was murdered by an intruder two years ago.

October 12: A couple is determined to have a Halloween themed wedding – describe the day, including the events, clothing, food, and activities!

October 13: A woman who is extremely superstitious finds herself facing bad luck scenarios everywhere she goes on Friday the 13th.

October 14: A security guard is working the night shift alone at night. Suddenly, there is a face in the basement staring at the security camera.

October 15: A group of friends go on a haunted tour of their city and take loads of photographs. In one of them they see the spirit of a little boy. Who is the boy and what can they do to ease his restless spirit?

October 16: A husband buys a doll for his wife from an antique store. They soon realize that the doll is haunted. What is the history of the doll? What havoc does the doll bring onto the house? How can they get rid of it so no one gets hurt?

October 17: A woman finally accepts that she is the last person on Earth. She settles in a vacant home – and there is a knock on the door.

October 18: A shopkeeper makes a special line of facial masks. The person wearing them takes on the personality of the mask.

October 19: A man wakes up to hear knocking on glass. At first, he thought it was the window until he heard it again - coming from the mirror.

October 20: A soldier returns home to discover that someone stole the dog that he had since he was a teen. He uses all the forms of social media to find his dog. Does it work?

October 21: A farmer builds a new home on a lot of land that once held a corn maze in the early 1960's. A 13 year old girl got lost in that corn maze and was found dead the next morning. The farmer's new home is now haunted by the spirit of the young girl. What does he learn about what happened that night? Is she an evil spirit or is she searching for something...or someone?

October 22: A film writer is working on a murder mystery loosely based on a true crime. He soon finds himself haunted by the spirit of the murderer who was shot and killed by the police in a foot chase, the day of the crimes. What secrets does the murderer have that the media didn't know and the families thought were buried with him?

October 23: A family moves into a home that has a room that is haunted by an angry spirit. But it is just one room! The family learns that the landlord's mother died in that room, after she was locked in there when she went senile.

October 24: A paramedic answers a call for help by a woman who was beaten with a baseball bat by boyfriend. His heart breaks for what she is going through at home. He slips a few comments in about how she needs to get out of the house and away from her abuser. When they part ways at the hospital he gives her, his business card and tells her to call if she ever wants to talk....and she does! Tell the story of how the paramedic tries to rescue her from the abusive relationship. Is he successful?

October 25: You wake up at 2:00 in the morning to go to the bathroom. While you are washing your hands you see another face staring back at you. Who is it and what do they want to tell you.

October 26: Write the last line from a horror movie and use it as the first sentence in a scary story!

October 27: A Halloween enthusiast has been invited to a middle school to tell the history of Halloween. What stories does he have ready for them? Now, write it in a way as if he were invited to a college to teach Halloween history.

October 28: An alien crashes onto a farm. What was the alien thinking and doing before the crash? Was he calling out for help?

October 29: A group of friends, in 1910, camp out in a field; waiting to catch a glimpse of Haley's Comet. Describe the events of the night. They each tell what they think is in the night sky beyond the moon and stars.

October 30: A millionaire gives his son the job of giving $100,000 to 10 people, groups, charities, or schools – he can only choose 10. Who does he choose, and why? His has 30 days to decide.

October 31: For 8 years on Halloween a woman finds a black rose and a small pumpkin on her car. She thinks it's adorable but her new boyfriend decides to investigate her friends and family to find out who is doing this – and why!

NOVEMBER

November 1: November is known as NaNo WriMo. That stands for National Novel Writing Month. Do you have an idea for a book that you always wanted to write? Now is a great time to do that! Remember, the challenge of NaNo WriMo is to write a book in 30 days!

November 2: If you could choose one of your friends to be president of the United States; who would you choose and why? What changes would they make in the world?

November 3: A local cooking school is celebrating, "Sandwich Day," with a contest for which student can create the best new sandwich! The judges are a group of firefighters. The winner receives a set of Aritsugu Chef Knives and a Breville bread maker.

November 4: A man falls into a coma after he gets a head injury from a skydiving accident in Arizona. His son brings an ancient Mayan statue into his hospital room because it is supposed to be lucky. He wakes up the next day – 117 years in the past. The hospital workers think it is just another day and that the man came in with an unknown head injury. The statue is still sitting on the table next to his bed. Where did his son get the statue? He goes to a local group of Native Americans to help him get back to the current year. Or can no one help him?

November 5: Rearrange or reword a cliché to start an article or story, for example...

"DON'T WORRY, BE HAPPY" to "DON'T WORRY, BE YOURSELF"

"THE CALM BEFOR ETHE STORM" to "IS THIS THE CALM BEFORE THE STORM?"

"EVERY DOG HAS IT'S TODAY" to "EVERY DOG HAS IT'S DAY~AND TODAY I WAS THE DOG"

"IN SEVENTH HEAVEN" to "ON CLOUD NINE IN SEVENTH HEAVEN"

"A DIAMOND IN THE ROUGH" to "A DIAMOND IN THE ROUGH – THE TEEN YEARS!"

November 6: Two men are in court for fighting. This is the third time. The judge sentences them to do community service at a homeless shelter. Write about the experience. What do they learn about each other?

November 7: A 911 Operator, who was abused as a child, is haunted by the calls of a little girl calling for help – the little girl is her younger self.

November 8: You have a neighbor that insists she has been reincarnated. What proof does she give to support this?

November 9: Interview an elderly friend/neighbor about their best memories growing up. Incorporate them into a story.

November 10: A teen who loves baseball buys a baseball from ebay that was used for practice by their favorite team. Tell the story of everything the ball has been through.

November 11: A group of men and women in robes are attending a ceremony at Stonehenge. Tell about the event.

November 12: What were the day's like for the first residents in your town? Write a story about it.

November 13: Write about an animal that saves a persons life!

November 14: What would you have for your dream birthday party? What gifts would you want? Who would you want there – if you could invite anyone?

November 15: If you died tomorrow, how would your obituary read? How would your best friend write your obituary? How would your enemy write your obituary? How would you want your obituary to read? Include everything that you always wished would happen for you.

November 16: High school seniors set off to collect quarters for a Christmas party for sick children but this small act of kindness turns into something so much bigger.

November 17: Write about a teen who makes a difference in their community.

November 18: Start a story with these words: In five years, will this matter...

November 19: The government is expecting a colony from another planet; that wants to make Earth their home. They must give someone the assignment of writing an instruction manual about how to live on Earth. They give it to an older married couple from the country and a newlywed couple from the city.

November 20: Every year there is a Cat Festival in Belgian. Cat lovers from around the world attend the festival which begins with a "Cat Parade!" Two friends win tickets to the Cat Festival. Write about their experience there.

November 21: You are preparing a meal in which the guests will be your idol and your worst enemy. What would you make for the meal?

November 22: A 14 year old girl spends the weekend trying to win concert tickets to see her favorite musician.

November 23: Write a story about the day in the life of a soldier during the Revolutionary War.

November 24: The Panda Bear was once thought to be a monster, a mythical creature, that most people did not believe was real. Now write a story about an inventor who sets a trap to catch raccoons and catches a baby Bigfoot. What would Americans learn about the Bigfoot after that?

November 25: Write about a time that you were raging with jealousy.

November 26: Did you know that the first Thanksgiving was actually 3 days long and they did not eat turkey? Write a story about the events of those days, as if you were there.

November 27: Write a first person monologue of a mom/dad shopping on Black Friday.

November 28: A little girl hates her freckles and rubs lemon juice on her face to try and get rid of them. Then she learns how her freckles make her unique and special!

November 29: Empty an old junk drawer and write a story that includes everything you find inside.

November 30: A wish that comes true, just not the way it was expected to.

DECEMBER

December 1: A waitress is given a lucky coin as a tip. It sets off a good and odd chain of events. The customer later returns to tell who he is and the history of the coin.

December 2: Two sisters are killed by a drunk driving when they were playing in the snow. They come back as angels. How do they change the lives the lives of those who need help, those who need to learn a hard lesson and of those affected by their deaths?

December 3: A story of how one random act of kindness sets off a chain of events that in time circles back to the first person.

December 4: An elementary school has their first "snow day" of the year and some friends get together to make "snow soup!"

December 5: Write about the first snowfall of the year!

December 6: Build a gingerbread house and write a children's story about the family that would live there.

December 7: President Benjamin Harrison was the first US President to have a Christmas tree in the White House. Write about the events of that day from the perspective of his assistant, the housekeeper and his children – Russell, Mary, and Elizabeth.

December 8: If the ghosts of Christmas past, present, and future were to visit you, what stories would they have for you?

December 9: If you could go back in time and witness, change or participate in 5 things what would they be? Why?

December 10: A deaf person attends a holiday party. Write about her opinions and judgments of the fellow party guests.

December 11: Write a story about what you think Heaven is like.

December 12: A blizzard comes through town, leaving 4 feet of snow and knocking out the power to every home for 9 days. How will the families spend that time?

December 13: Write an alternative ending to your favorite book!

December 14: A church youth group present their reverend/priest with an angel food cake, a gift bag and a handwritten letter of "Thanks." The gift bag has a small token from each teen. What are the items given and why are they special?

December 15: As a Christmas present for her family, a woman decides to create a book of 1,001 Family Facts and makes copies as gifts for everyone at the family Christmas party!

December 16: Write trivia facts that most people do not know but should know. Ask others for their favorite trivia facts. Create a children's story about a child who sets out to learn something new every day so when she grows up she can say "I know a million things..."

December 17: You are participating in your first snowmobile race and get lost. You see smoke coming from a chimney in the distance. As you approach, you realize you are in the North Pole – at Santa Claus's workshop. Describe the scene and the events during that afternoon.

December 18: An overzealous security guard at the mall is determined to catch shoplifters during the Christmas season – everyone is a suspect – in his eyes!

December 19: A teen boy has plans to he a writer, in fact, he likes to write poems. His father is against this and told him that if he does not go to college that he will take back the money that he has saved for his son's college tuition. His mother is in support of the teen following what he loves but also worries that he should have a more practical career choice and write poems as a hobby. However, they make a deal – if the teen can show all the proven and viable ways that poetry can be his life long career then his parents will give him the college fund to use for what he needs. If not, the parents keep the money and take a cruise around the world! He has 30 days!

December 20: Buy a wooden box from an antique store. Who could have owned that box when it was brand new? Where did they get it from and what did they keep inside of it? How did it end up at the antique store all those years later?

December 21: The brown stocking from the antique store was so old that there was a debate on its exact age. It didn't take me long to realize there was something magical about the stocking when I reached inside and pulled out _____

December 22: An angel is sent from Heaven with a message for you. What is the message and how do they relay it? Remember the angel cannot leave until you have received and believe the message.

December 23: A writer vows to enter every writing contest for a year! Does he win any of them? What does he learn about writing – and life – along the way?

December 24: Write about a millionaire who dresses up like batman and visits children in homeless shelters and hospitals for Christmas.

December 25: Retell the Nativity story, as if it were to happen in today's time period.

December 26: Doctors and scientists celebrated the first successful cryogenic freezing. He had no way of letting them know he was still conscious.

December 27: You find a book on a bus seat. Tell the journey of the book.

December 28: There is a tree in South Africa that is 2000 years old. It is known as the tree of life. If that tree could talk; what stories would it have to tell?

December 29: A group of friends are celebrating the New Millennium – the year 3000! How will they celebrate? What are their fears for the big 3000!

December 30: Make a Family Christmas Story. Write the first 2 pages of a winter/Christmas adventure book. Over the next year ahead, contact each family member and have each one write a piece of the book. For example, one of your cousin's write pages 3 & 4, a sibling writes pages 5 & 6, etc. Then you write the last 2 pages. Take your time, give yourself the whole year to complete the book. At Christmas time next year, make a copy of the book for each person that helped contribute!

December 31: A group of friends plan to get together on New Year's to have a "Toast to a Change." During the toast, they will each say something that they want to change or do in the upcoming year! There is one rule, it has to be something other than dieting or quitting smoking!

Other titles from Higher Ground Books & Media:

Wise Up to Rise Up by Rebecca Benston

A Path to Shalom by Steen Burke

From a Hole in My Life to a Life Made Whole by Janet Kay Teresa

Overcomer by Forrest Henslee

Miracles: I Love Them by Forest Godin

32 Days with Christ's Passion by Mark Etter

The Magic Egg by Linda Phillipson

The Tin Can Gang by Chuck David

Whobert the Owl by Mya C. Benston

Dear You by Derra Nicole Sabo

A Whale of a Tale by Uncle Dave Howard

Add these titles to your collection today!

http://highergroundbooksandmedia.com

www.ingramcontent.com/pod-product-compliance
Lightning Source LLC
Chambersburg PA
CBHW022133280326
41933CB00007B/670